Fearless & Flawless

My Healing Journey Through a 31 Day Fast

By
Lynette C. Norman

Table of Contents

CHAPTER 1: *The Knowing and the Lie* 10

CHAPTER 2: *The Knowing and the Power of Prayer* 12

CHAPTER 3: *Karma* 16

CHAPTER 4: *The Knowing and the "I Am"* 17

CHAPTER 5: *The Harvest You Plant* 21

CHAPTER 6: *Words-The Ultimate Game Changer* 25

CHAPTER 7: *My Story* 27

CHAPTER 8: *Radical Self-Love* 32

CHAPTER 9: *Healing Through the Process* 35

CHAPTER 10: *The Big "How"?* 39

CHAPTER 11: *My Why - Fearless & Flawless* 43

CHAPTER 12: *My Internal Shift* 45

CHAPTER 13: *You Can Do Anything (If you put your mind to it)* 48

CHAPTER 14: *Affirmations - Words of Change* 50

INTRODUCTION - A Fasting Journey: Self-Healing with Radical Self -Love

Fasting is a practice that has spiritual, physical, and mental benefits. Some people fast to express their love and devotion to God, while others fast to detoxify their bodies or lose weight. Fasting can also help you reset your relationship with food and appreciate it more.

There are several types of fasting, such as water fasting, juice fasting, intermittent fasting, and partial fasting. It seems like you are doing a partial fast, where you abstain from certain foods but still consume
some liquids and nutrients. This can be a
safe way to ease fasting and avoid some of the side effects of more extreme fasting, such as hunger, fatigue, headaches, and dehydration.

However, fasting is not for everyone, and it should be done with caution and guidance. Some people may have medical conditions or medications that make fasting unsafe or ineffective. Fasting can also trigger eating disorders or nutrient deficiencies if done improperly or excessively. Therefore, it is important to consult your doctor before starting a fast, and to monitor your health and well-being throughout the fast.

Here are a few other fasting guides:

31-DAYS OF FASTING | GENESIS Community Church: This is a blog post by a pastor who explains the spiritual and practical aspects of fasting for 31 days. He also provides some tips and suggestions on how to fast from something and fast for something.

DAYS OF PRAYER & FASTING - EFCA: This is a fasting guide for spiritual breakthroughs that covers the biblical basis, the benefits, and the methods of fasting. It also includes a 21-day prayer and fasting plan that you can follow or adapt to your own needs.

31-DAY JUICE FAST WITH EMILY- Juicing for Health: This is a personal story of a woman who did a 31-day juice fast and shared her experience, results, and advice. She also provides some recipes and resources for juice fasting.

WATER FASTING FAQ-Fasting Starts in the Kitchen: This is a frequently asked questions page about water fasting, where the author answers some shared questions and concerns about this type of fasting. She also shares her own experience and insights from doing several water fasts.

Many people struggle with food addiction, which is a form of neurochemical dependency on certain foods that can cause uncontrollable cravings, binge eating, guilt, and self-hate. Food addiction can affect your physical, mental, and emotional health, and it can be extremely hard to overcome. But there is hope. Food addiction can be treated with the help of professionals, support groups, and self-care strategies. You do not have to suffer in silence or feel ashamed of your condition. You deserve to heal from your food addiction and enjoy a healthy and happy relationship with food and yourself.

Here are some steps that you can take to start your recovery journey:
Seek professional help. A healthcare provider can diagnose your condition, rule out any underlying medical issues, and prescribe medication if needed. A therapist or counselor can help you explore the root causes of your food addiction, address any emotional or psychological issues, and provide you with coping skills and tools to manage your cravings and triggers. A nutritionist or dietitian can help you create a balanced and personalized eating plan that meets your nutritional needs and preferences.

Join a support group. A support group can provide you with a safe and supportive environment where you can share your experiences, challenges, and successes with other people who understand what you are going through. You can also learn from their insights, tips, and resources, and receive encouragement and accountability. There are many online and offline support groups for food addiction.

Identify and avoid your trigger foods. Trigger foods are the foods that cause you to lose control and binge eat. They are usually sugar, high-fat, or high-carb foods that stimulate the reward centers of your brain and create a cycle of addiction. You may need to process how to eliminate these foods from your diet completely or at least limit them to special occasions or controlled portions. You can also replace them with healthier alternatives that satisfy your taste buds and nourish your body.

Practice self-care. Self-care is essential for your well-being and recovery. It involves taking care of your physical, mental, and emotional needs, and doing things that make you happy and relaxed. Some examples of self-care are getting enough sleep, exercising regularly, meditating, journaling, reading, listening to music, spending time with loved ones, and engaging in hobbies. Self-care can help you reduce stress, improve your mood, boost your self-esteem, and enhance your quality of life. You have the strength and courage to make positive changes in your life. You are worthy of love and respect, from yourself and others. You are not defined by your food addiction, but by your unique and beautiful personality.

You can do this!
I believe in you!

Food facts

The impact of food on nations is a complex and multifaceted issue, influenced by a wide range of social, economic, and environmental factors. It is important to recognize that while food has the power to nourish and sustain populations, its misuse, mismanagement, and unequal distribution can indeed have devastating effects on societies. One key aspect to consider is the role of food insecurity and malnutrition in contributing to poverty and social instability within nations. Inadequate access to nutritious food can lead to widespread health issues, hindered economic development, and social unrest. Additionally, the unequal distribution of food resources, both domestically and globally, can exacerbate disparities between diverse groups within a nation, leading to societal tensions and conflicts.

Furthermore, the impact of industrialized agriculture and food production on the environment has also had profound consequences for nations worldwide. Deforestation, water pollution, and soil degradation are just a few of the environmental challenges linked to modern food production, which can have far-reaching implications for the stability and sustainability of nations.

Considering these complexities, addressing the issues surrounding food and its impact on nations requires a holistic approach that incorporates sustainable agriculture, equitable food distribution, and social and economic policies aimed at reducing poverty.

Consuming food is essential for life, as it provides the energy and nutrients that our bodies need to function properly.

Some of the most important benefits of eating healthily:

- It keeps our heart healthy by lowering blood pressure and cholesterol levels(12).
- It reduces the risk of developing some types of cancer by providing antioxidants and other protective substances(13).

- It improves our mood by influencing the production of neurotransmitters, such as serotonin and dopamine[1].
- It supports our gut health by feeding the beneficial bacteria and preventing infections[1].
- It enhances our memory and cognitive abilities by supplying essential fatty acids, vitamins, and minerals[1].
- It helps us maintain a healthy weight by regulating our appetite and metabolism[1].
- It prevents or manages diabetes by controlling blood sugar levels and insulin sensitivity[1].
- It strengthens our bones and teeth by providing calcium, phosphorus, and vitamin D[1].
- It improves our sleep quality by affecting our circadian rhythms and melatonin production[1].

These are just some of the many benefits of consuming food, especially healthy food. Eating well can also benefit our environment, our society, and our future generations.

I wish you all the best on your fasting journey!

1: Benefits of eating healthy: Heart health, better mood, and more 2: Benefits of Healthy Eating | Nutrition | DNPAO | CDC 3: Health benefits of eating well - Food and nutrition | NHS inform : [How food can improve your mood - BBC Good Food] : [The Gut-Brain Connection: How Gut Health Affects Mental Health] : [Brain foods: the effects of nutrients on brain function - NCBI] : [Healthy Eating for a Healthy Weight | Healthy Weight, Nutrition, and Physical Activity | CDC] : [Diabetes diet: Create your healthy-eating plan - Mayo Clinic] : [Nutrition for Healthy Teeth - Mouth Healthy - American Dental Association] : [How Food Affects Your Sleep - Sleep Foundation] : [Why is healthy food important?]

CHAPTER 1: *The Knowing and the Lie*

<u>Discipline must come from within; true self love is discipline. (Radical Self-Love!)</u>

Self-talk; at the refrigerator:

"Why do you hate me so? Why are you making my flesh scream from stretching and self-indulgence?
Why do you hate me so? What did I ever do to you Lynette? Why do you talk so ugly to yourself? WTF?!?"

The repetition of self-hate that comes from self-abuse repeatedly, is the main reason we fall and cannot pull ourselves out of any pits of destruction.

WHY can't I stop being this emotional punching bag to myself?

WHY ARE YOU EATING THAT AGAIN?!? Why can't you keep from overeating and engorging?

Why can't I stop the cycle that has been embedded in my DNA? If I could eat my way to success, I would have been the winner years ago!

This self-hate that was stuck, rooted in me in the dark abyss of my soul, the core of my being. I believed the lie, and the one who told that lie was me! YES, ME!

I believed NOTHING pure or beautiful about myself. I was my own victim! So, guess what? I would eat, eat again, and eat some more because of this self-perpetuating lie.

I listened to the inner voice that said you are and never will be. I let it run my life every day for years. Which, in turn, forced me to have these negative thoughts throughout all my life situations.

But I always had my back up plan, FOOD. I liked to serve it up with a little cup of stress, a plate of self-hate, accompanied by a little dash of the fuck its.

So often I would create this river of gluttony so that I could float down it in my bowl of ice cream, covered with marshmallows and tears of self-hate running down my face.

When life let me down, I had food. When it was a rare time for celebration, I had food. The comfort I would get from shoveling these unwanted calories in my own face, became the reward. It was one of the only things that I was able to control. The temporary satisfaction that I offered myself. Yet food was merely a jumping off point for a torturous journey of self-soothing.

It became the start of a life full of addictions from drugs to alcohol, porn and sex.

Giving up on these selfish habits, selfish desires, and physical cravings, releasing the hold from my addictive personality traits has been the game changer for me. It enabled me to become the true I AM within me. It has allowed me to find my inner self and connect with the source of my spirit.

Throughout the process of fasting and inner healing, I have realized that by sacrificing oneself, come the promises of universal law and love. It is a way to better one's inner being, with love and chastening.

CHAPTER 2: *The Knowing and the Power of Prayer*

Learning your words

<u>Prayer:</u> *An open communication window, time, or space where you send any type of message to your higher power or higher self, with any use of nonverbal words or verbal words that are sent into the universe for guidance or favors, blessings, healing, and any other desires.*

Growing up, whenever we were with our grandmother, the religious powerhouse that she was, she always impressed upon us prayer before we ate, no matter where we ate. Yes, we are that family that bows our heads before we eat anywhere.

Giving thanks is the most beautiful response and compliment you could ever give a chef or household cook and your heavenly father.

I was so shameful when I bowed my head. I felt a sense of embarrassment. I was sure that everyone was staring at me, judging me. But to be honest no one cared! It was a lie that I would continually tell myself. I realize now that it was my Ego.

I was on a non-stop route on the self-abuse bus. That was my reality. It was a learned behavior. Something that I thought I deserved, and at that point in my life, I didn't know any different. It was a result of the abuse that I suffered when I was younger, and the abuse continued because I CONTINUED IT.

Simply put, THE ABUSED, ABUSE! LET ME SAY IT AGAIN! THE Abused ABUSE. Your DNA has traits in it from generations of old. Patterns are created from past experiences, and appear in many different forms: verbal, physical, sexual, emotional, etc. Sexual abuse is one of the most common forms of abuse nationwide. The number one sin is that it has been covered up over multiple generations.

Remember the death of Abel? Cain, Abel's brother, killed him, and Abel's blood screamed from the dirt where it fell. I want you to see how powerful your blood line is. The traits that become part of your lineage, have been molded into the very fabric of your being. Research suggests that trauma can directly affect a person's DNA. This can potentially impact the health of future generations.

Abuse can come down to something as simple as marriage. As a society we are told that a man and a woman are supposed to marry and have a family. Marriage has been forced upon us, shoved down our throats. Driven by tradition and faith, the expectations placed upon us as women causes us to fear the consequences of not "falling in line". This is a type of abuse. Even worse is that situationally behind closed doors and drawn curtains, this fear filled abuse to submit to a husband or a religion, is socially accepted.

This is just a fragment of the abuse that I suffered, the fear that was embedded in me and a driving force that aided in the abuse that I, in turn, caused myself.

We push through this abuse all day long. We make the excuse that it is human nature. Why can't it be stopped? Why can't we stand up as people of abuse and say, "FUCK YOU!" heal and move on?

Let me tell you why. It is because we are trapped within this habitual fallacy that has been embedded into our DNA. We dizzy ourselves by consistently cycling through a web of tangled lies. We take the torch of abuse from our abusers and ultimately become abusers of ourselves.

We have openly listened to this lie of previous generations, whose ABUSE CHAIN has become their way of life. Their mental health, sickness, and disease and consequently added their links to our own abuse chain.

Humanity has been trapped within these habitual lies. Deceptions that have torn apart families, divided marriages, perpetuated fabrications of ancestral history and certainly worst of all, have stolen the innocence of own their children.

This generational theft is of yourself.
<u>Self-Abuse:</u>

It is easy to get lost in the habitual lies surrounding self and self-worth. When you exist in an environment where abuse is the expectation it becomes very self-deprecating. This causes many adverse reactions. It all leads to the same thing: not knowing one's true self and minimizing their worth.

The lie that one's abuse is deserved and justifiable, becomes the foundation for a life full of destruction and the excuse to keep abusing oneself.

My mother is a perfect example of self-abuse and how that can transmit to those around you. My mom never knew who her real father was, and it was something that she was never able to get over. This one aspect of her life manifested so much hate within her. This one event hugely changed everything in her life. The dishonesty made a shift in my mom to where she forgot about her own kids. And what is neglect? One of the most reported forms of abuse.

She was so entangled in her situation she forgot about her own kiddos. She ignored her parental responsibilities. Her self-abuse transformed itself into her neglect of us. And as the abused abuse, I wound up doing the same to my own kids.

Within me was a ticking time bomb, and I too went down a dark path of self- hate and destruction. I created the same world for myself just like my mother...Fuck, I was her!

Not by choice but by Karma.

Your words have such power! What you say to other people, how you respond to anything and especially what you tell yourself. It can be your greatest tool or your weapon of self-destruction. I wish she could have known about the power of words. Fuck if I could just show her now!

Show her that she was always loved. Perhaps, had she known that she was loved, she would have been able to love herself. I loved her, and I did not even know how to love.

Mom's experience was self-infected, until she was able to seek the help she needed later in life (which I am so blessed to say she did before her passing that was just over a year ago). Dad loved her until the day she passed. He never remarried. Magic, right?

Love is such a magical thing, and self-love is where it all starts.

I am in love with healing, restoration, and the obsession of mad crazy, LOVE.

CHAPTER 3: *Karma*

Kare about your actions, all actions *(Thoughts create action)*
Action your next move will cause a reaction. *(Words)*
Reaction is caring about your memory. *(Power is in the memory)*
Memory keeps your previous action in the forefront of your mind. *(Thought)*
Action management response to Karma. *(Ultimate power thoughts)*

Karma is real! You may have asked for forgiveness or healing from actions from the past, and you receive that blessing and healing, BUT there is still a universal debt owed to your DNA, and we all must pay. That is the law of karma, the law of your human suit.

True healing comes from seeking clarity from your past, not dwelling in it. We are never meant to stay in those moments of old, where lies live eternally. They are the lies that keep each one of us in a state of doubt. Any thoughts of doubt that become planted represent that first mental seed. That first seed is what starts your forever life garden.

The absence of a guidance system is when people appear as if they function as humans yet exist with no emotions aside from reacting to their own frustrations and fear. Fear and frustration then transform to anger, destruction, and resentment. None of these emotions support love and healing.

Love is where the changes come. Loving yourself is how to start the process of healing. Healing is only done within a place of self-love.

The journey of life is ever changing, that is why it is a journey.

CHAPTER 4: *The Knowing and the "I Am"*

The "I Am" finding.

If we open up and allow the healing process to work and to be successful within us, we will become the "I Am" within us. *(The "I Am" is the name of the spiritual self, as distinguished from the human self.)*

Going through life and never seeing it with open eyes, being so blinded by Ego, is the ultimate death sentence that we give to ourselves. Not being conscious of your thoughts, your words and your environment can easily cause your mind to "fill in the blanks". The mind is such a powerful thing that if you cannot see who you truly are, it takes control and creates a life for you! Relinquishing control of your negative thoughts and following the path of self-abuse will result in being controlled by a different master, the Ego. Once the Ego has been given the power to control thoughts and actions, your search for the I Am in you becomes that much more difficult.

The only way to true, everlasting success is through finding the I Am in you.
Finding the I Am in all situations will give you the lens you need to see the universal world through Gods' eyes and the God in you, the I Am.

I am the beginning truth and light and the first and last.

The shift that changed me was when I realized that the abuse bus was real. Fuck, I had been on that joy ride for years, without even looking back. Stuck on the highway with a rearview mirror that was beyond delusional.

That is when I would investigate and reflect. My whole life had been driven by this man-made fear. I latched onto that fear like a nursing infant never wanting to let go, not knowing when I would latch on again. Everything I knew was in that rearview mirror and fear prevented me from focusing on what was ahead of me.

Looking back and seeing the chapters of life that I lived and having watched the pages turn every day into a self-created story has been so jolting. Why would I ever want to create this world of self-hate and destruction repeatedly for myself?

Emotional punching bag:
When you beat yourself up over the same thing repeatedly, leaving self-made scars.

It is easy to fall into specific patterns. Depending on your story, hearing, and accepting the ugly things are easier than receiving words of encouragement or affirmation.

Self-abuse, like making yourself your own emotional punching bag, or even an emotional punching bag for others, is a common example of how we exist in a world of self-hate, self-abuse, and self-destruction. However, when proper guidance is given, when instruction comes from a place of love it allows for a changing of the heart. This transformation is when we see amazing examples of humans creating super humans who are honest and pure of love. And this change allows us to see the Gods and Goddesses that we are in ourselves. We are the I Am in ourselves.

Over each journey in my book of life, there have been countless jolting, life changing moments. I was so blinded by self, that I did not even recognize these moments (not the "I Am" in me; I had no clue what it was at some points in my life, I was just pure self and pure hate). It took me a while to realize that the hate wasn't coming from within anyone else, but, that the hate was in me.

The blame game was so strong within me. I was the "accuser", and it gave me fire to make every day a day of self-abuse. I put myself on the rollercoaster of self-made Hell. It was self-created and was so fucking toxic! I allowed myself to lose everything repeatedly and on so many self-loathing occasions. The reason why? Because I was so focused on self, the flesh of self. My own skin had become this trap of abuse and lies, but most were self-made lies as a manner of self-destruction. The truth is I was my own "self" killer!

Pure selfish:
A selfish action that only you see self in, and an action that only helps your selfish ways.
Pure:
An action that values oneself with the utmost self-love, respect, and purity of heart.

The lie that I had listened to over the next three decades made me see that, once you are fully consumed in self, you slowly forget the I Am in you, and you wind up abandoning self-love. The result is everything transitioning into selfish intentions with no remorse.

When someone is in a self-destruction mood, they only see through tunnel vision. Everything else around us fades because we are living amid self-made delusions, lies, and deception. Believing that you have nothing or will not be nothing is one of the biggest lies (other than that we are not loved) we tell ourselves as humans!

Convincing yourself that you are not capable of being loved or loving others is the lie of all lies. YOU ARE SO LOVED, and I love you as well. So please, stop lying to yourself!

This first lie we tell ourselves usually starts from the first mistake that we make as humans. This lie is so crippling that for generations it has taken our humanity as individuals, and it has had a ripple effect on communities.

The song we sing to ourselves on replay is what we become. The words we use to describe ourselves, the phrases we repeat in our minds, the mistreatment of us and the misconceptions that we hold onto all prevent us from being our genuine selves. They deprive us of being our "I Am".

Finding who you are is going to be the most important, life altering experience you can have in your human suit.

Self-talk:

How you speak to and about yourself. How we speak to ourselves can be one of the most damaging forms of abuse. For me it only comes second to marriage and the church (they are the absolute fucking first!).

Your words have a spiritual reflection, and the reflection it has on you, is the reflection of faith that you have in yourself.

The power behind me is greater than any power ahead of me! That power is your WORDS.

Finding your voice and hearing is the only true way to have a complete relationship with the I Am in you. And the only true way to have that radical self-love. It is the only way you will find the I AM in you; faith comes by hearing.

The realization of this has been life changing! When you hear someone speak, and you truly tune into their words and receive some kind of benefit from it, that is spiritual growth. Any kind of growth has a spiritual reflection on its actions. We may not see it at first, but when you start this shift, a spiritual knowing is given to us. The universe opens her blessing upon us and whoever your spiritual guide is, they are right next to her cheering you on! You already have a fan club!

CHAPTER 5: *The Harvest You Plant*

Self-doubt is the seeds that have been sewn into the self without conscious permission. They stem from the words of others. The seeds can be harvested later in life through your everyday actions, or they remain unharvested until the time of abuse is uprooted through your way of life and thinking.

The example that comes to mind now is having dyslexia. Growing up, I was not given the tools I needed to learn and thrive. Whenever I was given any help or guidance, I was so fearful that I pushed it away. I did so, not realizing what damage I would end up causing myself. I let my Ego be my God and I became its puppet. It was my master, and as such I relinquished all control.

This was the excuse I used to be lazy with myself. And by allowing myself to be lazy, I had given myself a reason to not be accountable. The lies we tell ourselves because of our egos or persona, are fucking rattling.

Grandpa A

Grandpa A taught me how to spell using basic flash cards when I was around eleven, and these cards are still in my grandma's hutch. Crazy!!!!

I had beautiful handwriting and learned how to write in calligraphy. It was one way to keep eyes off the learning disability and let my God (my EGO) be in a higher place than the I Am in me.

The self-hate I had was unreal. I can feel that angry little girl sometimes still, BUT fuck! I love her so much! Now I can see her, hear her, and embrace her with so much love through this healing process.

I struggled with the persona of these visuals, thoughts of fear and hurt, and then made those into Gods as well. It became a way of life for years.

I became a visual learner only at that time. I was terrified of reading and math; I was bullied and hated life. I dropped out of school because of fear.

I got expelled in middle school for getting into a fight with a teacher and ended up at an Esperanza school for pregnant teen moms. I dropped out after I got into a fight with a girl at school and then moved in with my grandma. I was fourteen and pregnant.

I wound up moving from my grandma's, which I regretted long after. I beat myself up for years for being a horrible mother. I could have stayed, and I would have been safe with my son.

I let my EGO lie to me. I allowed my persona to be my fucking guide, holding my hand through eyes of a beaten and battered child.

I had no clue or any idea on how to be a parent, I just wanted to love: be loved and give love.

During this time is when I learned about my past and that there was a chance that my dad was not actually my dad. I felt betrayed, I was around 14.

My grandma did not tell me that my dad had been gone for 6 months before my mom got pregnant. I am not sure why she didn't, but she didn't!

Maybe it was because my dad did not care that I wasn't biologically his. He loved me regardless and I was his no matter what. I do not know. But I used that excuse for years and used it for self-abuse as well.

I did self-create a superpower though! I could watch anything one time and make it or copy it, but, if it had anything to do with reading, it was a non-stop joy ride on the fear bus of self-abuse. I was poison-to myself and others.

My grandparents eventually had to step in, and they took us from my father. My dad didn't always make the best decisions, but he did the best that could with what he had.

My beautiful Auntie B would fly in and always save us. She even went so far as moving to CA to help my dad. He needed her help. He was just so lost. I was around 10 when I moved with my grandma, for the next few years.

They were my unsung heroes in my life, my grandmother and Grandpa A, my eyes were covered with a veil of lies and self-hate. Lies of a little girl who was so bossy and hurt.

I had no clue who I really was, but my grandparents were my safe zone, I knew that much.

My grandma, the bad ass that she was, took us and made it work with no extra help. She took three kids who had been so neglected, and she tried to give us the first real stability in our lives. She was trying to erase the wrong that had happened to her and her children. All she wanted was to protect us and I did not see that. I was so blinded by my woes, wounds and mourning of my childhood. I was stuck in a state of pure selfishness.

My Grandpa demonstrated and offered me pure love through his actions. It opened my eyes to wanting to learn. I had been terrified for years because of bullying, but I was so fucking hungry to learn!

He made my education his last wish. He knew he was dying, but he loved me so much. His last concerns on this earth were teaching me. He needed me to know the most important values in life and love.

It almost killed me when he passed away, and I never looked at death the same way again. This damaged me so much. His death was my excuse for years of losing the I Am in me. It played the largest part in my actions of being a fucking ass hat and starring in the lead role of victim and expert manipulator.

I acted out and became this ugly human after my grandpa passed away. I was a broken, shattered girl. Not knowing how to read and on top of that having ADHD and Complex PTSD cause my life to shift.

The times I felt safe were with my grandparents. They would pick us up for the summer and that truly allowed us to vacate our lives. We had food and clean sheets and no lice. We traveled. I was able to live through a different lens focused on the beauty of life.

We went to the beach and would experience life for a week. Sometimes we would even pick up my sister, Heather. That was the best time ever!

My grandpa worked so my grandma would just live her best life with us. My grandpa was my true hero.

Then we would be thrown back into reality. We would be back to my dad and his brokenness. My dad tried so hard being a single man with scars that striped his back, and three damaged kids who just wanted to be loved but did not know how to be, because of the abuse that he had already experienced.

My dad broke the chains of abuse later in his life. I have been able to see where the shift happened for him. He saw that his ego needed to be broken, and we spoke about this on many occasions.

I became the mother to my little brothers and a bossy one at that (ego). But no matter what, my love button for everyone else was real.

Fell madly in love with cooking and nature, and then slowly I forgot about his passing, my grandfather.

I listened to the lie that he was the only one who loved me, and that's when rebellion started. The bus stop created in my mental warehouse had begun. This was the beginning of so many bus stops that over the years I have had to change these specific stops. These memories must be brought into captivity!

Through all these reflections of life, I have been able to open my mind and pinpoint where I walked away from the "I Am" in me.

CHAPTER 6: *Words-The Ultimate Game Changer*

Learning the power of words has been a game changer! Affirmations really work and do so because of the hard wiring in them.

The same is true for words that are unspoken. Hate can be blasting in one's head without one word being uttered. And when action is put behind these self-delusional thoughts, one action can change the history of one nation. Hitler is a fantastic example: pure selfishness wrapped up with self-delusion.

Self-delusion is letting no other voice be heard, but your own, and your ego is your true God.

That my love is true selfishness, and self-love twisted into hate.

THE TRUE POWER OF WORDS

It is said that faith comes by hearing, and in the bible, it says by the word of God. Where you plant your seeds, YOUR words, and decisions, create each chapter in your life! They are the pivotal change that we all seek and yet cannot find!

And your ego is screaming at me and this book right now, Run far away! Fuck the truth hurts! The opening of one's spiritual ears can be extremely challenging, and that is because we do not have faith in our own knowing.

The seeds we sow:

When potting a plant, you remove all the old soil, break it up gently, then loosen the roots up with a loving touch, protecting them, trying not to break them or damage them. If needed, you would lovingly cut back the roots to a healthy spot and re-plant in new soil leaving just enough room for growth.

<u>Do not</u> plant your seeds in a huge pot with no substance! When you repot a plant, you should never do so into a pot that's more than three inches bigger than the previous pot. It is too much room!

Plants like to be rootbound. Roots need to be grounded yet rooted deep enough in the soil. With too much space around the root, they will slowly die. Not enough space, they will suffocate. There is a sweet spot. It is the same for us.

The spiritual reflection is the same for us if we're in a similar situation. If in a pot that is too big without our root system being strong enough, we will slowly suffer from some type of root damage. In a spiritual reflection it would be not enough substance and we would suffer deprivation on every level. We become sensitive to all movement because there is no substance for root support.

Making the conscious decision to nurture your roots and promote your own growth is where the shift will start. It's a development of trust within every single corner and crevice hidden within you. The shadows where fear has kept healing captive. And true healing is the pathway to spiritual freedom. It is where you start to see the real glimpses of the "I Am" in you.

That is how fucking powerful your self-love environment is! Fill your space with what you want to see in your life, what you want to become and what must change to release that inner badass! Change only comes by action.

CHAPTER 7: *My Story*

When I was 14, I ended up pregnant with my first child. My grandma was so mad, and my Ego did not understand why. I was happy! I would have someone to love and someone who would love me back. My dad was happy (he was still drinking then). It seemed crazy, but he was happy. My Ego ran about with the fact that he was happy, and I listened to the lie.

Right before I had my son, my grandma and I had the only fight we would ever have. The fight that broke me as a human!

Please understand that my grandma was an angel, but she was hurt by my smartass mouth. She had every right to be pissed at me.

During this heated discussion, my grandma informed me that the man who I had been told was my dad, was NOT actually my dad. I learned that my mom was beyond promiscuous, and let dreadful things happen to me as a child.

The impact that this new information had on my spirit was immeasurable. The words infected me like a virus and my decisions redirected, my priorities reorganized. I too, would abandon the priority that was my children. I learned from my example. I was bound to repeat a cycle: *the abused abuse!* I was on my way to ending up just like her!

This is a demonstration of the power of words. Something that is spoken out of anger, a promise that has been broken, lies that are told. All are idyllic examples of the true power that is harnessed in our words. And that power is world changing.

A call that changed my life:

August of 1993:
The first version I heard was that my mom's mother, my grandma B, called and was told that her son, Bill, had a six-

month-old daughter that needed someone to come get her. I was unwanted. And she did not want to take care of my mom's mess.

My dad's version was different. He said that my mom got a hold of him, he had no clue how she found him, and I was about 6 months old. When he met me, he fell in love with me immediately. He said at that moment his life was forever changed. He stated that I was blue because my mother had a rare blood issue (this conversation update happened on February 27, 2024).

My grandma Snuni had her own version which was completely different. She said she got ahold of my grandma B when I was being delivered, and that my dad's family was aware of me.

By this time, I honestly stopped caring. I was on the third version of how I started out in this life, and I just felt so lost. The common denominator in all the versions was simple: I was hurt by my mom's actions.

I was my mom's middle child. She had her first baby when she was fifteen and had me when she was twenty-one. My mother had also been married twice already but was unfaithful. When she got pregnant with me, she was still married to my sister's dad. It seemed pretty apparent that determining who my real dad is was not going to be so cut and dry.

My dad tried to create a relationship with my mom because he loved her. She was a beautiful, exotic Jewish mix. All he wanted to do was take care of me and my half-siblings. He loved her, he married her, and he tried so hard to create a marriage with value, but he wasn't perfect. The "iron fist" mentality crept upon him with my oldest brother and us kids. My mom called CPS on him for his reaction towards discipline. Please remember: *the abused abuse*. My dad took classes and broke that chain of physical abuse. (Unbeknownst to us, mom was already having an affair again) He shifted his energy, and his healing came.

The day I felt the most LOVE was when my dad said to me, "Who else was going to take you?" I did not feel hurt or attacked by him when he said that. I felt so much love. This broken man who had suffered his own demons, chose a little girl he had never met. And he did so, knowing that I was not his.

Thank you, Dad! I would not be here if it were not for you and would not be able to share my love story with the world. I love you, Dad!

The hell started when my dad left.

By the time my dad finished all his classes, my mom moved on and moved us kids to her lover's back yard to live in a tent. YES, A TENT!

My dad found out where we were staying, and he helped my mom get a house. Around this time is where he disappears temporarily, and the time when the abuse starts on a different level. I was with my mother for only a few years, my dad took us once he got his life kind of back on track.

To this day, my dad regrets the way he was he has not drunk alcohol in 31 years. He has asked for forgiveness and shed many tears because of it. He was misinformed or the information was misrepresented. The guidance he received about marriage was marinated in hate and fed to him on a religious platter. Shit rolls downhill, right? I adapted and adopted certain ideals. The fear of sin that was forced down my throat, and the illusion of a marriage being a place of safety, is what dictated certain aspects of my life.

I had my first child at fifteen.
I was married at fifteen.

The rest of the phone call went like this:

Basically, it came down to the fact that my mom needed help, and that Bill should step up and take care of me. So, he did!

My grandma shared many stories with me that day. She vented to me about her own abuse she endured. Stories about how she was forced to marry the first go around. However, her next two husbands absolutely loved her! Her chapters of love stories are such magic.

Please understand my grandma was my safe place, my everything. So, when these words came thrashing at me in anger,

I knew in that moment, I shared something with my grandma. It broke a part of her that I never realized until later in life.

I wish I had a chance to say sorry and try again. Fuck, I wish! I self-abused over this whole conversation and let it eat at me for years.

My grandma was big on fasting and living a "fasted" lifestyle. Thinking about it now, I fast so often because I feel like it brings me closer to all the little moments I forgot about later in life. It's been pure magic!

The story my grandma shared was out of anger, but it was true. We all have our own side to a story, but the timing sucked. I let it wrap around me at that very moment. That is when the lie became my ideal and my golden excuse. I used it to obliterate my world without even knowing it.

This was the key to my next few chapters of life.

I ran with the idea of not being wanted, not even knowing if it was true! It was my way to self-abuse for the next 20 years. I never asked anyone on my mom's side if this information was true because I had the self-made impression that I was not loved by any of them. I let my persona become my guide at that very moment, and my Ego be my driving force to my own self-made self-destruction. The pity-party I felt became my new ruler for all life actions and choices. I let this party rule my life for years

Reminder:
"This space is a safe place; it is a place of self-reflection.
No matter how bad it is,
this is the only rightful place of healing.
And that is in the space of love."

Forgiveness is the only true way to healing, and forgiving yourself is going to be the only way to true self-love.
"Always keep FORGIVENESS at the forefront of your mind, please do not let it EVER slip away, be thankful for forgiveness every day, because when you stop that is when we forget and overlook what we once had done, and we end up jumping on that fucking bus again."

CHAPTER 8: *Radical Self-Love*

The only true way to heal oneself is by healing their inner child. The average person would have gone into mourning over this conversation and started the preparation for this cycle of a pity party without invitation. It is an unwanted and unforeseen universe of hell that is self-created.

True self abuse, at its' finest, is being that emotional punching bag once again. By this time in your life, your bag is only being held together with duct tape and zip ties!

Over each one of these chapters, I shared with you the cycles of self-abuse, and abuses that were active in my life.

Fear was the number one driver for me. I had this devil complex that if I did anything wrong, I would go to HELL or if I did anything wrong, I could ask for forgiveness. It was a way to justify self-abuse. I was already healing from the abuse I endured for years! I went on these cycles surrounding the love of God and different faiths. I studied LOVE and all of God's love for all humanity.

I love learning about the love of God and His love story of healing. I fell madly in love with this idea of true healing with insight and knowledge. I fell in love with the promise of mental freedom from the affliction I had pressed upon myself without knowing that I was doing it.

"*My children parish for a lack of knowledge.*" God is talking about knowing that we are our own true God, this is our temple, and we need to love and honor it.

I was raised in vineyard churches, and I was filled with the holy spirit and power. I started praying in tongues at an early age. I lived a fasted life on and off throughout the abuse I inflicted on myself.

What changed me was radical self-love. I figured if I was expecting change, I had to do it within.

I started studying Gods' love and the love of all religions. I learned about the Gods and Goddess. I studied Reiki and Hinduism and then went on to study yoga and meditation in all forms. I went down this rabbit hole of self-healing. I knew I needed to change and shift my energy into healing. I knew about these amazing healing modalities, and I wanted to see where my energy would go with a self-made idea of a healing fast.

I was not attending a church when I did my first 31 day fast, nor do I attend now. You are your temple, and church should be held within you through any healing modality.

However, I watched churches participate in a specific ritual at the beginning of the year. The whole church would fast and bring the new year in with a clean slate. They would fast for guidance. They would fast for spiritual growth.

Through fasting, radical self-love planted a seed inside of me, and the growth was undeniable. I embraced this change. I wanted it more than anything.

This is how I looked at it: if I was so willing for years to let my ego be my boss and dictate my every action, then why not do the opposite? Why not make a radical change through self-love?

And this is where my true LOVE story begins.

Finding oneself through the turmoil of the past can be tricky, because in all actuality, we really have no clue who we are and where we belong. We have an intuition and an idea, but truthfully, we have no fucking clue! We have opted for deletion. We observed the reality show we starred in daily as children and planted those seeds. They then become the harvest that we reap as we get older without knowing It. Become conscious of this and realize the power in your thoughts and words is what changes the world.

Every human needs a foundation to stand on. One that is pure to self and self-supporting. That foundation imprints the most crucial decisions in your life. If we habitually make patterns that are unknown to us because of our lack of self-knowledge and love in our inner self, we subconsciously put ourselves in a self-destructive mood. Because of the power we have, we have no clue that the words we speak are not only the seeds for our future harvest, but they are our current harvest.

CHAPTER 9: *Healing Through the Process*

Self-healing and Self-love:
The window to the soul is through the journey of healing and self-love.

Over the last few years, my personal healing journey has been a roller coaster of absolute craziness! It has been the most challenging journey that I have been on to date. I cannot even express the joy and love I have now. I feel like it is going to bust from my inner seams, and this energy light is going to pour out of me with a shimmering glow of beauty! I have this energy force that is so strong within: Quantum Radiant self-love!

I learned to love myself through the process. This journey could take a few trips, or it may just take one solid rattle to shake you up. Nonetheless, it is your journey!

Please hear this: know that we all fall, we all trip and stumble. We may even scrape our knees along the way. These battle wounds are not to hold you back. They are to teach you to move the fuck on and let your healing work for you!

Healing through the process is where the magic happens. It is within that remolding, refining, and in peeling away the layers of the onion. It hurts a shit ton because we are having to face ourselves; to break conditioning habits that have adhered to us. We take these habits; Make these discouraging life decisions based off conditioning that was given to us from our abusers. Or we were influenced by the church and spiritual teaching. The lies of submission!

What may have worked in the past, which was based on a man's word and fear driven, does not work here now. As we are a species of growth and change, so must our ideology.

The best decision I ever made was stepping away from the religious lie of the "MANufactured" church. I released myself from the grasp of people who let these abusers hurt their children and ultimately away from a church who supports it.

Disclaimer: Please note that I do not believe that all Churches are corrupt! I love Churches, I have attended hundreds of services. And have been spiritually fed on all levels.

REMINDER: IF YOU ATTEND A CHURCH THAT APPPROVES OF OR PROMOTES ABUSE, YOU ARE AN ABUSER AS WELL! If you let harm come to another human or if you know of it yet don't say or do anything to stop it, you are just as guilty.

For years we let the elders in the church hurt and molest our children. We turned a cheek, listened to the lies of a man. We put trust in the sources of these lies and allowed our fear to justify it.

It took years for me to break this human-caused fear of HELL (and self-made hell). I tried for years to have relationships with men, yet always had an underlying fear of them because of the abuse I went through. It was pushed on me from the beginning. I wasn't given the choice.

I had to do what was said or told. I was not allowed to be gay or have a mind of my own. I was instructed to have kids, get married, go to church and to live my life in fear because my God was an angry God. He will send me straight to Hell for my actions. This fear almost killed me on more than one occasion. I sacrificed my true self because I was so fear driven. When you are driven by fear for so long, it takes a little while to work out the old ways of conditioning. It will not fix the issues overnight; I'd be lying, if I said it did, and you would automatically lose trust in me. You know the truth within, and having that knowledge, is what has you reading this book. Fuck, it may take a few years BUT the healing process is so worth it!

The growth spurts will hurt just like when you had growing pains as a child.
This pain caused from healing the self comes from within. It is what lets you know that positive things are being accomplished, and the transformation is functioning.

Being able to heal from this pain is so intoxicating that we start to crave the healing processes.

The same can be seen when it comes to spiritual reflection: *Energy moving.* The shift in energy is different, and it supports us on a quantum level of healing. It is worth the mental freedom alone.

The process that I have taken over the years has helped me shift some mountains in my life and blow others up! I like to call it, *"I do not give a fuck what you think!"* I AM NOT a victim any more or a slave to my own ego or self.

Giving in or giving up on your old self is not quitting, it is evolving, and growth is the only place for change.

If you do not like you then change it. It is that simple. Yes, the truth is, it's going to hurt, but fuck! Think about who you have hurt on your way to become who you are now. Think about the abuse that you've suffered by your own hand.

CHAPTER 10: *The Big "How"?*

I started evaluating my inner self and ultimately investigating me. Something was not sitting right within me, and this internal battle needed to end. I was slowly killing myself with abuse and self-hate. I was being suffocated by the fear of not having an understanding. Any type of learning situation showered me in dread because of my struggles with Dyslexia. I was tired of this false version of me.

I knew my love for God was where I needed to start this journey. I reflected on being filled with the Holy Spirit since I was a girl. It helped give me a new understanding and a foundation to start this radical self-love shift. Not only within my life but most of all, within my spirit.

I prayed, asked for my eyes to be opened spiritually. For the universe to open her heart to me and to shower me with insight, knowledge, universal understanding, and to send the right humans my way to help me learn. To send Sages and teachers to open my heart. I prayed for true inner healing on a Quantum Radiance level, and it worked! I found my voice that day. I found the true power within it.

We all can see my love for God. I will never push my God on you. I will show you *my* faith in Him. How I have survived myself and the lies I've experienced in the world of religion. How I absorbed other religions and fell madly in love with them. How I have learned to honor and respect all Gods and Goddesses.
"Knowledge is key to all success; my children perish for a lack of knowledge." -Jesus

After learning that the Bible is a spiritual tool for us to use on a mental level and is meant to be a guide for the spiritual battlefield of the mind, I embraced it as such.

Joyce Myers "Battlefield of The Mind" is a beautiful place to start a foundation on your spiritual thinking. This book is one that I studied when I did a Rhema Bible School course.

My studies have been amazing, I have had so much fun learning about Hinduism and Judaism, Buddhism. I personally practice a little of all faiths. I would say I am a lover of all faiths, and most beliefs. I respect them all and honor them by sharing some of their practices.

There is so much beauty in each belief system. For example, let us look at Reiki.
Reiki is a healing energy technique. What an amazing practice! The focus is to shift energy through your body to heal it. I always called it "healing hands". I have been practicing this method for 20 years and it works! I believe the reason it works so well is because it is a healing method that focuses on self-love and mental healing. You must be in the right state of thinking for this practice to work.

Tapping EFT Emotional Freedom Techniques
Gala Darling has been my teacher for a year now and I pay for her classes (remember the best investment is in yourself). Spending your money on your mental health is the number one gift you can give yourself.

I tap my "karate chop" the most. If you are a victim of abuse and tapping triggers you, tap your karate chop and allow it to change your life. The power in this healing modality is stellar and it works. You learn to trust yourself through this process and it changes your way of thinking. You think constructively. You learn that it is ok to forgive yourself and love yourself through your process. I love it!

Reconditioning your mind is the most imperative thing you can do for yourself. Start by fasting social media. There is no reason for an adult to be scrolling mindlessly on a device, and certainly not if it doesn't feed your mind on a quantum level. If it isn't teaching you something valuable, then it is not worth your time. This mental investment will take time so, be patient with your amazing self.

Cathey Heller: my Jewish Princess
Cathey has opened herself to the world by sharing her journey of success. What a powerful story! I am so in love with her personal love story. If you have not listened to it, please, give it a shot. It will give you a whole new outlook on the magic of love.

When I think of magic, Cathey comes to mind. She is a Goddess. A little songbird who sings her songs through shifts of energy; her words are spoken from true knowledge and understanding. Her knowing and faith in herself, pure magic. I press more into her work for the spiritual side.

I will put this out there: she is the only person I have considered asking to be a personal coach and I would pay anything for her time.

Joe Dispenza
I have pressed into Joe's ways of meditation, and they have just blossomed my spiritual understanding and seeing. The spiritual reflection of energy in this field is mind blowing on a quantum radiance level.

The inner shift comes from the knowing of the "I am" within you and that you are your own God. This is your temple and how you treat it will shine through on everything you do in life.

The recognition of the mind is the real game changer. But it takes practice, and it will take a few years just to create a new foundation for growth.

Joe's way of thinking and ways of self-correction hit the nail on the head.

Jay Shettey
The man with the perfect questions. The consideration that Jay displays is pure love. His works are done with no intentions other than love. I feel his energy and his shifts during his podcast; the way he listens with open ears to his guests. Jay displays pure love lead by action, through mediation and positive thinking.

Jesus
 I love the bible. Learning that it is a book for mental health was a game changer for me. The stories in the bible are not to be driven by the fear caused by the lies of man and the Church. The Bible was written to be a guide for our mental journey.

 Some of my favorite books that I read last year. I love audio books and highly recommend if you do not have time sit and read a book, listen to one on your drive to work or during a workout.
<u>Seth Speaks</u> – Jane Roberts
<u>Abraham Hicks</u> -Ask and It Be Given- The Law of Attraction
<u>Louise Hay</u>- The Power is within You- You Can Heal Your life -I Can Do It
<u>Gala Darling</u> -Radical Self Love; High Vibe Honey Tapping- I am part of her community.
<u>Deepak Chopra</u>- 7 Spiritual Laws of Success
<u>Florence Scovel Shinn</u> -The Power of the Spoken Word – The Magic Path of Intuition – The Game of Life and How to Play it.
<u>Neville Goddard</u>- Awakened Imagination

CHAPTER 11: *My Why - Fearless & Flawless*

Love is my WHY! Over these last few years, I have fallen in love with life and humanity in such a way that change came without much hesitation on my part.

The seeds you sow will always grow; we are the reflection of our spiritual harvest.

I realized when I pulled my head out of Pandora's box that the chaos of the world would change. I was looking at the world through a different lens, one on a spiritual level, through a quantum level window.

Daily reflection is the only way to shift to a higher level: through meditation, fasting or prayer. I adopted this reflection habit around 5 years ago, and really started focusing on it as a success tool. Reflection is a tricky place because we are taught to reflect on our actions, our bad habits, and then we are pressed to change that habit without any true guidance or tools of success.

The fear of God was pounded into MY head, and the result of that action lead ME down a path of self-perpetuated, fearful ideas. I constructed my own hell on top of the spiritual hell that man created.

The tools of success have not been given fully to us *because* the Bible has been tampered with so much. Books have been added in-along with fear.

Please note I am NOT saying the Bible is the only book of importance in the universe. What I am saying is: the book that was pressed upon western America was stated to be the most important book in the world. That is why we have followed it for generations. We have allowed the fear of God and Hell to rule through it and over us.

The lie that churches must be paid for your survival and protection is what feels so damning. The Bible was intended to be used as a success tool for guidance and direction on every mental level. That pure intention has been veiled by man and made into a death sentence for those who don't follow the "rules". Man has taken this beautiful guide, the most valuable human-caused guide in the universe and made it into a book of fear and judgment.

With this God, man's God, we are made to suffer for anything and everything. If you make any mistakes in life, you are damned and will never make it to heaven. So much fear! I was living under this illusion of outer-worldly Hell and Hell on Earth, and I could not do it anymore. I had to change and shift my energy into something else.

I started with my self-talk and anytime I began an attack action, I would correct it right away. The ultimate power is your words and shifting them is one of the most important actions you can take in your life. Within your words you possess a strength and that is why the church has tried to steal them for centuries. Your words are your power, and we need to stand up and not let anyone take them again.

I am here to help you change that. With love and guidance from your inner "I Am", you can change your world internally and externally. You can shift into the new you as simply as changing the chapter in this book.

I hated it when I would hear someone say, "It is that simple!" It would make my skin scream and my mind crawl! Such words I will not say! FUCK!

After this self-transformation journey that I have been on, I can speak with absolute certainty that the power is within you and me.

CHAPTER 12: *My Internal Shift*

My internal shift started by changing my words and actions. I speak to myself as I would want someone to speak to me. My self-corrections are soft and loving. If you abuse yourself repeatedly this may be tricky, especially if you have an ugly vocabulary, but can all start by changing your words! The power words of success start with "I Am" statements.

I start my day the same:
I wake up and shower in the dark, I meditate, and I do a little shower work out.
My phone stays in my office and I do not look at it for my first 1-2 hours of being awake. This is my time, and I am extremely selfish with it.
I wake up early every morning because my internal alarm clock says, "Get up beautiful! Let us get ready for the world and this day!" This tunes into the knowing that my internal presence needs to be awake and needs to be in tune just as much as my external presence. We are a team.
The main reason for the internal shift I was seeking was, I did not want to live a life in fear anymore. I needed to end beating myself up over my daily actions. My own self judgment was so crippling.
I needed a change! I did not want to come home from work, hang out, drink, and waste my life away. I needed more than to watch every TV show known to man or get lost in the mindless chatter of people not providing me with enjoyable conversation.
I do not spend time with people, and that is by choice. I speak freely and most individuals cannot handle that. Honesty is what we all crave, but what most cannot stand to hear. I end up giving them free information that they may not be seeking. Yep, I am known for that gift!

I have learned that walking away is the best action for me. It is because of how much I love myself that I do that. I will not play any mind games; they are pointless and only hurt all involved.

I have learned what works for me. I respect that and I honor myself through these actions, my self-made actions.

Standing up to and for yourself is where the real battle is. Reframing and reconditioning your mind can be challenging. It can only be done with self-love and love driven actions.

The reason why it can be so difficult is because it took years for us to get this way. Expect that it will take just as much-if not more-time to heal your inner child.

We are ass hats to ourselves and fuck, the only true enemy you have is yourself. We are our own worst enemy and that's a fucking fact! If someone does not like you, it does not make them your enemy. It makes them human, and they have every right to their own understanding.

You are your own abuser. Yes, you may have been abused, but we are the ones who perpetuate that first action. We choose how we clutch or relinquish that action of abuse.

Now the shift you are seeking is here and available to you. You must want it bad enough to change. Remember a few little seeds can produce a harvest big enough to feed you (and anyone around you) from the overflow of abundances.

Trust each time that you take an action step, change will come. I knew within that I had taken the right action step for this next journey in my life. I knew that the shifting changes were the beginning of the end to years of mental bondage.

I started small and worked toward my desire to become the best human I could. It was the first time I worked toward my own desires and not someone else's!

Trusting in yourself is the overall goal. Once you can learn that your inner voice is your guide, your intuition can help you with knowing that you are the master of your domain universe. This is when the change will come.

Your strength is built up by love and inner change with radical self-adjustment.

Adjustments come from day-to-day changes. You may not see them clearly at first, but you will see them once you start. You see your new world through a different lens. Meaning when you shift your energy and vibration into the spiritual side of the playing field, the change will come.

Trusting who you are is the most important thing!

CHAPTER 13: *You Can Do Anything (If you put your mind to it)*

I showed myself how to trust me, my inner knowledge and how to tune into that knowledge. I believe that we have a foundation that is already within us, and we turn a blind eye to it because of fear itself and the fear of change.

We all have been blessed with DNA traits and imprints that have been left on us from others. They can be spiritual and physical (good or bad!). What we choose to do with that is purely up to us. We have the freedom to make our own choices. There are situations where freedom may be taken because of the control of another person, but that will change no matter what. Change always comes, growth is inevitable.

After I studied and meditated on all the questions that were running through my beautiful mind-and with lots of prayer- I have concluded that we are the creators of everything around us. We manifest life experiences from joy to self-made hells. IT'S us!

I started watching my every word that came out of my mouth except for "fuck". I have had a case of the "fuck it's" the last 10 years.

I made corrections. I am always the first person to say sorry and change my actions. I realized that I was the person who could set myself free. I released myself from the religious lies of man and my own lies of the ego and persona.

I started meditating and I uplifted my prayer life! I realized my every action had a reaction. I started intently looking for these human glitches within. If I felt that my reaction to someone was fueled by selfish intention or self-seeking action, I stopped at that moment. I reevaluated and rethought.

It has taken many years combining ample opportunities, time, and space to perfect these habits within myself. To be honest, there has not been one day that I have not been excited for these internal changes and spiritual shifts. I will NEVER get tired of it! I now crave growth and change.

I have realized my place here on this planet, and it is to serve humanity; to have an attitude of difference.

I openly speak of my daily victories (even if it is just learning something new about myself or something that I may have pressed away in a former life). I embrace all my personalities with the utmost respect. Every mood I have is part of me and my inner being, and I fucking love that about myself! She is a Queen among Queens and Goddess among Gods.

The magic we hold is beyond words or experience. You must use YOUR words to make action happen, to create the inner magic you seek. The guidance you are looking for is within you. I will help give you the tools for success, but you must be the one to make this happen.

Find one thing that I have mentioned in my self-recovery and start implementing that action in your life.

I have done it through fasting. I have done it with self-talk, and I have done it with action to reaction awareness.

I have done it by drinking water, by self-awareness with words, and by waking up just a little early for self-reflection time and prayer. I have done it by just reading a book on mental health, by sitting here and reflecting on my life story with you. I have done it by learning how to breathe and how to trust my own breath. I have done it by learning about the love of my God and all Gods. And ultimately, by just loving myself through my daily actions.

We are the grace and love that we seek in someone else. Yes, this human suit may get lonely, and interaction with others is very important, BUT you are the most important daily interaction you can have.

I know that you can have everything that you ever wanted, it just takes work and steps to get there (a steady step).

CHAPTER 14: *Affirmations - Words of Change*

I am the daughter of the King, the walls of decay crumbled away!

I have known the power of words since I was a little girl, but I was never taught they are to be used for good. I was told that you create worlds of negativity from your words and actions. That God hears everything, even your most intimate of thoughts, and you will be judge accordingly for each thought. I was told that God would condemn me for having any immoral thoughts.

Fear had been served to me on a golden platter, and I ate it up. (the same way as my face shoveling). Fear was my God for years. I was driven by fear and a lack of knowledge because of dyslexia. My lack of understanding at that moment in my life helped me create a backdraft of life events, self-created hell. My words only plunged me into the deeper chasms of that hell.

The true power is in your wagging tongue. Thoughts are powerful but only with action. Words put action into place. They foster mental, physical, and emotional movement. That's what is so disastrous.

I said for years that I never wanted to be my mom, which I wasn't really, but I did go down a dark path that resembled her life (all the way down to the number of kiddos we had). I was so scared of becoming her, that I slowly started to.

I remember telling every human I could that I would never be like her, and here I was setting my shoes into the footprints that lined her path.

I listened to the inner lie within me: that I would never be anything or amount to anything because I was just like my mother. And I slowly got this impression of her without even genuinely knowing her. A prime example of how things embed into your DNA. YOUR DNA DOES NOT PLAY!

Everything my younger self truly hated I became. Actions lead by words are magic no matter what the choices. Regardless of if the outcomes are good or bad!

I had to stop saying powerful words about myself because I was terrified of them. I understood what was being told to me, but the fear that was driven inside ate me up, spit me out and sent me tumbling down a path of self-destruction.

There was a point in my life that I was so scared to even speak because I had listened to lies that were being said within my own head. I created this world that was so amplified and deceiving.

We are everything that we seek: if you look for success you will have it. If you look for hell you will create it. Being able to establish this knowledge with purity of heart has been so gratifying. What you put in the universe will be created. It may not be at that exact moment in time, but it will come to pass. If you say that you are in the dark, then you will be. Enlightenment comes from knowledge and from hearing. The key to your universe is knowledge.

I am the affirmation within myself that I seek.

Until you speak powerful words over yourself you will stay stagnant in your own grounding. You are the success that you seek.

You can see the power in words from the imprint your parent(s) left on you as a child. If they repeatedly said you were going to be successful, you are more likely to be. If they spoke words of failure over you, then you most likely struggle being successful. The result depends on what you planted: the seeds of lies and hate they spoke over you or the seeds from words of love and growth.

Love is the only way to change. You can shift and change and be a success story, but if your foundation is not built on love, your success will ultimately fail.

One of the truest failures in this life is not loving oneself. It is because love is the only way to true healing on every level of life: spiritually and emotionally and physically.

You are your own self-reflection so, reflect TRUE LOVE!

Personal note to my readers:

"I absolutely love my life, and I am beyond grateful for my love story, the "I am" in me. Thank you for letting me share it with you, I love you all so much. One day I will hug you and share my love of my inner being with you. AND if we cannot meet up someday soon, please pull from my energy of love for you, and the universe and I will be with you. Knowing you have somebody in your corner no matter what, is what you have with me. For those who know me from a past chapter in my life, I hope that you see the growth and self-love I have created here for my ultimate healing and radical self-love."

Love,
L.